THE
TWO-STEP

THE TWO-STEP
The Dance Toward Intimacy

Written by
Eileen McCann

Illustrated by
Douglas Shannon

Grove Press
New York

Published simultaneously in Canada
Printed in the United States of America

Library of Congress Cataloging-in-Publication Data

McCann, Eileen.
    The two-step.

    1. Intimacy (Psychology). 2. Interpersonal
relations. 3. Intimacy (Psychology)—Caricatures and
cartoons. 4. Interpersonal relations—Caricatures and
cartoons. I. Title.
BF575.I5M33   1985   306.7   85-14764
ISBN 978-0-8021-3032-7

Grove Press
an imprint of Grove Atlantic
154 West 14th Street
New York, NY 10011

21 22 23 24   19 18 17

For Peter, who taught me to really dance.

My deep thanks to Michael Rosenfeld, for the opportunity.
My thanks to Doug, for the vision and the hard work.

CONTENTS

Introduction 1
Seeker and Sought 5
Power 32
Distance 54
Switching 78
Intimacy 101
New Steps 125
Really Dancing 147

FOREWORD

We are standing at the edge of an evolutionary leap where the prevailing nature of relationship, namely that of a fixed leader and a fixed follower, is being seriously challenged. This pattern of relationship has encouraged misuses of power and reinforcement of dependency, allowing for only "conditional intimacy" and punishing vulnerability. Within this form human beings have to behave through force and defensiveness, wear masks, have physical illness and hide low feelings of self esteem.

Since we have come to realize that all persons need power, intimacy, and a safe context in which one can be vulnerable, the prevailing pattern of relationship works against what human beings need. This amounts to a lethal war within us which exacts great tolls from our bodies, our minds and our hearts. In order to belong, we train ourselves to present our "should" face or mask to the outside world, thus giving false clues to others about who we really are. Then we punish others for not understanding us or punish ourselves for not being valued. It is no surprise that there are so many relationship casualties when we consider the ways in which we divide ourselves.

Relationship is at the very heart of human concerns. We can change our relationship and therefore affect the way we cope with our concerns. We are discovering new ways to relate which can reverse the casualty count. The first is choosing to honor our respective needs for power, the ability to stand on our own feet, make decisions on those things which affect us, and to have the courage to say our real yes's and no's. The second is to develop intimacy, a condition in which we can experience feeling seen, heard, understood, touched, and accepted, and to offer this to another. The third deals with the creation of a context in which one can express one's vulnerability, revealing our doubts, fears and weaknesses, without fear of rejection or punishment.

The means to all of this lies in our willingness to communicate, to share what is in our hearts, feelings and minds. Relationships which live in these new ways are strong, vital and positive. Issues and ego needs are not as likely to get mixed up. Self worth is high. There is no need to hide. The secret is out. We are all human.

Within this kind of relating, the inner needs for connection, for recognition, and for mattering can be congruently manifest on the outside so one can truly feel seen. One no longer needs to divide one's self. Instead of feeling diffused and tense, the self can be focused and a sense of confidence heightened. This applies to all personal relationships.

The ingredients of constructive pairing are the same. The same can be said of destructive pairing. Within non-personal relationships the essence is the same, but the words may be different. Power would be more labeled as responsibility and accountability, intimacy labeled as trust and good will, and vulnerability as honesty.

Our inner being has always longed for a new kind of way of being with another. However, we lacked the permission to express it and to act on it. What we need now is to give ourselves the courage to act on what we know.

Until relatively recently there was no hope of actualizing these longings, since it seemed like such an individual affair, so they were kept inside and festered or died there along with the person. Permission for becoming more fully human is popping up in all kinds of places. We now have more "permission" to discover ourselves, to enjoy ourselves, and to develop dances between us that are stimulating, fun, harmonious and productive.

I find this book to be a pictorial treasure of how we act, showing the games we play, while trying to hide what we want. Out of these pictures comes a clear realization of what we are doing. With that realization, we can laugh at ourselves and be inspired to make the changes we need to make.

Virginia M. Satir

INTRODUCTION

Why do all couples have such a difficult time becoming – and remaining – close?

We all have one thing in common – we follow the steps of a dance which keeps us from getting what we say we want from each other in our relationships.

It's a dance in which we use our everyday problems – fidelity, money, sex, children, drugs, jobs – to struggle over these issues:

...Power...

...Distance...

...and Intimacy.

It's called the Two-Step; we all dance it in our important relationships, whether as mated couples (straight or gay), as friends and lovers, as parents, children, and siblings.

Stumbling around on the dance floor can be dangerous to our happiness. In these pages you'll recognize yourself, your partner, and the steps you've followed in your Two-Step. You'll also learn some new steps. I hope they'll make you more expert on the dance floor, and happier in your relationships.

THE
TWO-STEP

Every relationship is a dance
with two roles being played...

...the
SEEKER...

...and the SOUGHT.

One is always in pursuit,
the other on the run,

no matter
how close...

...or far apart
the dance
may be.

This Two-Step happens
between lovers,
straight or
gay...

...parents
and
children...

...siblings
and friends.

The SEEKER is the "good guy" in all the love songs, books, and movies. The world applauds and encourages the SEEKER.

The SOUGHT is the "object of desire." SOUGHTS get plenty of attention, but very little compassion or understanding.

SEEKERS and SOUGHTS have very different ways of feeling about themselves.

The SEEKER feels
turned on...

...accepting...

...sexual...

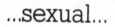

...committed...

while the
SOUGHT feels
disconnected...

...critical...

...neuter...

...indecisive.

Then too, the
SEEKER is
rejected...

...wanting...

...needy...

...and
victimized...

12

while the
SOUGHT feels
desired...

...superior...

...untouchable...

...and abusive.

SEEKERS see themselves as good guys and victims – the other guy is always wrong.

They feel the bittersweet pain of being "in love," yet rejected.

SOUGHTS feel guilty for rejecting. Others desire them, but they keep questioning their own worth.

They feel unloveable.

Most of us have played
both roles in our lives.

You may be a SEEKER
with your lover...

...and a SOUGHT
with your kids.

Maybe you're
a SOUGHT with
your best
friend...

...and a SEEKER
with your boss.

But chances are
you've played the
same role...

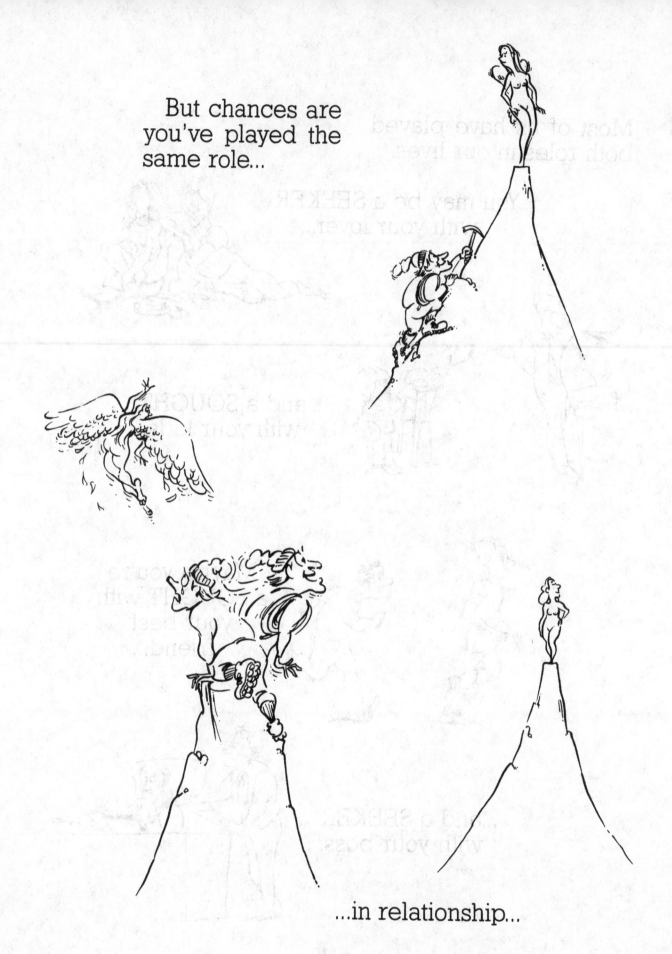

...in relationship...

...after
relationship...

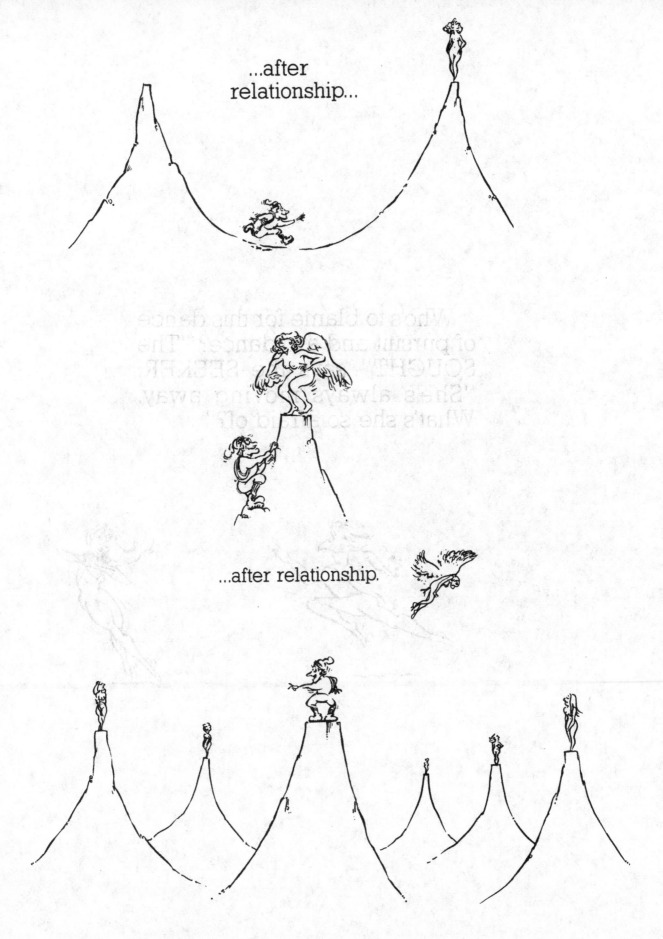

...after relationship.

17

Who's to blame for this dance of pursuit and avoidance? "The SOUGHT," says the SEEKER. "She's always moving away. What's she so afraid of?"

The SOUGHT is afraid of
being overtaken...

...overcome...

...conquered...

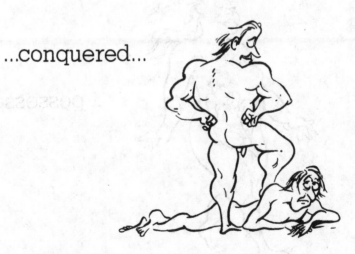

...smothered...

...sucked up...

...possessed.

SOUGHTS are afraid of being weakened...

...molded and manipulated...

...left without
identity.

Even as children
SOUGHTS felt invaded.
Care and affection seemed
to be pushed upon them.

The SOUGHT learned
to protect...

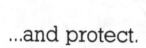

...and protect.

The SOUGHT is afraid of **SURRENDER!**

For the SEEKER, nurturing
and attention were
often withheld.

The SEEKER
learned to please...

...and please!

The
SEEKER
is constantly
on the move –

– giving,
initiating, and
manipulating.

The SEEKER is also
afraid. He's afraid that if
he stopped seeking no
one would seek him.

The SEEKER is
afraid of being unwanted.

Fear drives both
dancers in the Two-Step.

SEEKERS, in their
fear of loss...

...SOUGHTS, in their
fear of surrender.

As we do our moves we
trigger each other's fears –
fears that keep us from
feeling safe with each other.

Out of our fear
we vie for
POWER.

Power can mean who's on top?

...or who
gets
their
way?

Some power struggles
are very basic.

36

Other power struggles
grow more complex over time.

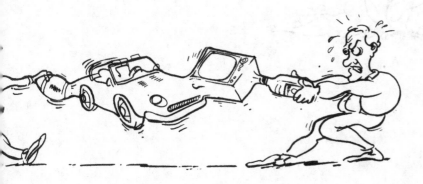

Some feel power
in conquest.

Others find power in thinking they've chosen beneath themselves.

There is also the passive
route to power.

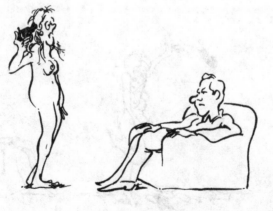

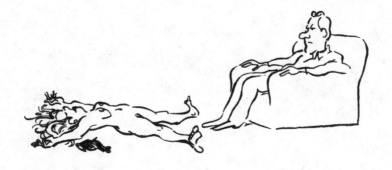

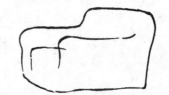

So which one of us has
the power in the dance?...

...who controls
the Two-Step?

Is it the SEEKER?
He's got all
the moves.

Yet it's the SOUGHTS
who can say "NO."

Unfortunately for
SOUGHTS, "NO"
is sometimes all
they can say.

Is the SOUGHT in control then?
YES...

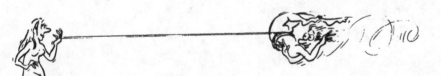

...as long as the
SEEKER keeps
seeking!

Both dancers maintain their own control. Every Two-Step has its own unique balance of power.

When one of us starts to feel controlled by the other's moves it brings up old fears...

...fears that can turn our dance
into an endlessly escalating
struggle for power.

Fighting for control is
not the only way we deal
with our fears of the other.

We also use distance
to keep us safe.

You can create
your own
space...

...define your
territory...

...put up a smokescreen...

...or a front.

You can hide away...

 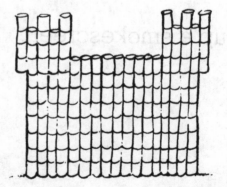

...or drift away.

We may be meeting needs for little
distance with an office in the home...

...or needs for lots of distance by
working different shifts.

Who creates the distance
in the Two-Step?...

...the
SEEKER...

...or the
SOUGHT?

Some SOUGHTS run at any possible signs of seeking...

JANICE, THIS MAY SOUND CRAZY... BUT I'M DREADING MY BIRTHDAY. TURNING THIRTY HAS ME FEELING ANXIOUS.

SOMETIMES I WONDER IF I SHOULDN'T JUST SETTLE DOWN AND MAKE SOME BABIES.

WHAT?! ARE YOU KIDDING? YOU WANT TO JEOPARDIZE YOUR CAREER?.. YOUR FRIENDSHIPS?.. YOUR CARELESS IMPULSES??

SOCIETY'S MORES ARE CHANGING, DAVID. YOU DON'T NEED TO PROVE YOUR WORTH BY CASTING YOURSELF IN THE SAME MONOGAMOUS PROVIDER ROLE AS YOUR FATHER!

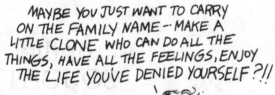

MAYBE YOU JUST WANT TO CARRY ON THE FAMILY NAME -- MAKE A LITTLE CLONE WHO CAN DO ALL THE THINGS, HAVE ALL THE FEELINGS, ENJOY THE LIFE YOU'VE DENIED YOURSELF?!!

BUT....

FORGET IT DAVID! I'M NOT GOING TO MARRY YOU!!

...and there are SEEKERS
who jump at any sign
of distance.

There are SOUGHTS
who know how to
hang in close...

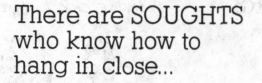

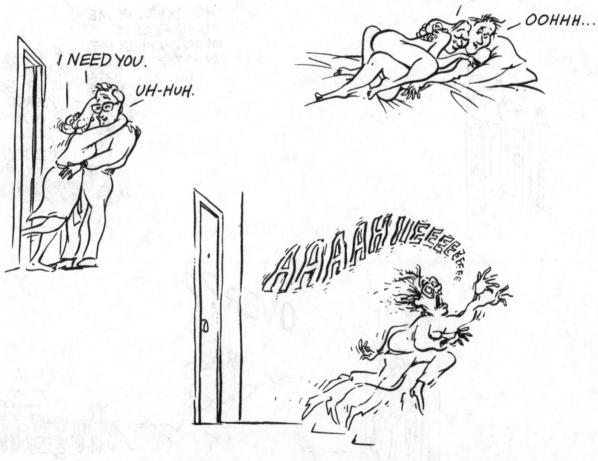

...before they
need to run.

64

...and there are SEEKERS who only seek from a safe distance.

JAY, YOU'RE REALLY SPECIAL. YOU REALLY DO UNDERSTAND WHAT I'M SAYING.

OF COURSE I DO, JOHN.

I NEVER THOUGHT I COULD SHARE SO MUCH OF MYSELF WITH ANOTHER MAN— —BUT I TRUST YOU!

I FEEL THE SAME ABOUT YOU, JOHN.

WE'VE GOT TO GET TOGETHER AS SOON AS POSSIBLE!

WHY, OF COURSE... ...WE MUST..

JUST AS SOON AS THOSE BARGAIN FLIGHTS COME BACK I'LL WING IN FOR A WEEKEND, WHAT'YA SAY?

SOUNDS PERFECT!!

There are SOUGHTS
who only need to make
small moves away.

THAT DOES IT!!

SEEKERS and SOUGHTS tend to blame one another for moving too close or running away.

However, we are not the victims of our partners' natures. We all, even SEEKERS, need some distance in order to feel comfortable in a relationship –

– and we are always dancing with someone whose needs somehow match our own.

For example, in relationship after relationship, although our roles may change, we find ourselves the same distance from our partners.

Very early in our relationships a distance is established...

...and that distance
usually stays the same.

Just as power is shared,
distance is mutually
maintained.

SEEKERS look as though
closeness is all they want...

...but they
move in rhythm
with the SOUGHT'S
steps away.

SOUGHTS look as though they just want to be alone...

...yet they pace themselves with the SEEKER'S pursuit.

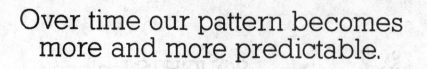

Over time our pattern becomes
more and more predictable.

We run the dance
into the ground.

For our relationship to be viable,
alive, and open for contact...

...the roles must
SWITCH.

The SEEKER can
feel **wanted** when
he is finally pur-
sued.

The SOUGHT can
feel **wanting** when
she has room to move.

If dancers switch roles – and switch often – a tired or destructive relationship can become alive and vital, even if it isn't always pleasant, easy, or fun.

Maybe we've been seeking
for three months...

...two years...

...or fifteen.

How destructive must our dance become before we switch roles?

(and not simply partners?)

Switching roles can be a
scary step for both of us.

When SOUGHTS find themselves with room to move they discover new unexpected fears.

SOUGHTS don't know how to take the initiative.

They feel awkward and clumsy...

...unsure of themselves in the role of the SEEKER.

And when SEEKERS are finally pursued, their new role fills them with fear too.

SEEKERS are uncomfortable being receptive...

...unable to control the pace.

SEEKERS get nervous with nothing to do.

We felt more comfortable playing our old roles – even though they weren't getting us what we wanted – we felt safer.

The SEEKER felt safe
as the desperately
wanting victim.

The SOUGHT
felt secure as the
rigid rejector.

What both fear most
are the responsibilities
of an equal relationship...

...where the
SOUGHT not
only receives,
but also gives.

...where the
SEEKER not
only gives, but
also receives.

It only takes one of us to initiate a switch –

—but playing the other role and hanging in past the moment when our fears are most intense is very difficult.

The SEEKER can't fake the role of SOUGHT.

OK, I WON'T SAY A WORD. TONIGHT HE'S GOING TO COME TO ME!

CHICKEN'S TASTEY.

ISN'T IT THO?!!

I GOT THE RECIPE OUT OF THAT NEW) A BLAH HSC) IT BLAH ECIT+NC ECOIY BLAH NUI SKI9 DBLAH 4SN NAI CAI BLAH KINONE MIRZ TIOIT BLAH LMR BLAH BLAH BLAH..

THINK ILL CATCH THE NEWS

92

THIS IS
RIDICULOUS

IN ANOTHER
FEW MINUTES
SHE'LL FOLLOW
ME IN HERE, TOO

I'VE GOT TO OPEN
UP, DAMMIT! I'M
GOING IN THERE AND
TELLING HER HOW I
FEEL. I'M READY
TO DO IT-- I'M GOING
IN THERE AND SHARE,
SHARE! SHARE!!

The SOUGHT
can't bluff the
role of SEEKER.

93

When the
SOUGHT has
a change of
heart...

...and makes
her first
hesitant
steps of
seeking...

...what will
she do when
the SEEKER
creates the
tension...

...that makes
her want to
run again?

And when
the SEEKER
finally gives
up the chase...

 ...and tries
to become
the pursued...

...how long will he
hold out when the
SOUGHT disappears
from view?

Our fear in giving up our old roles is that our partner won't switch with us.

IF I STOPPED PURSUING SHE'D MOVE AWAY AND LEAVE ME ALONE!

IF I STOPPED DEFENDING
HE'D GLOM ONTO ME AND
OVERWHELM ME!

What we need to trust is that out partner will keep dancing with us...and will switch to keep in step with us.

For the SEEKER, switching roles means having enough self-respect and integrity to stop seeking.

It means being aware enough of his limits and needs...

...to be willing to become...

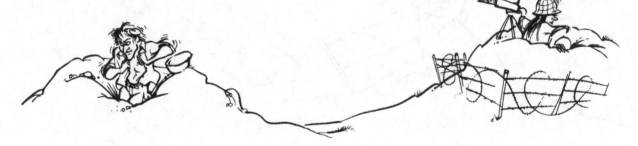

...a SOUGHT.

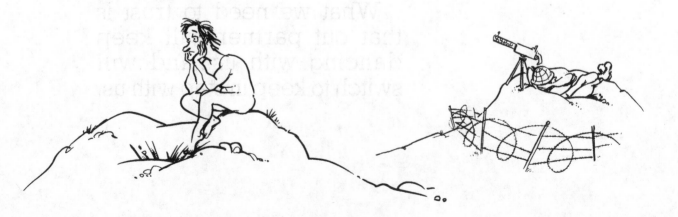

For the SOUGHT, switching means wanting the other enough... ...needing the other enough...

...to become aware enough of the other's importance in her life.

...that she is willing...

...to SEEK.

Facing the fears of loss and surrender we become truly vulnerable, appreciating the risks of the other as we do our own. As we share each other's vulnerability at the same time we achieve **intimacy**. That's what the Two-Step is all about.

Intimacy is two people being **exposed** at the same time, showing the good and bad parts they usually keep hidden.

Intimacy is two people being **vulnerable** at the same time, trusting each other with the parts which can be hurt.

Intimacy is two people simultaneously **seeing** and **being seen** by the other, fully aware of their vulnerability, with the intention that their dance will continue.

Intimacy is the moment when we let go of our old patterns of pursuit and rejection...

...when we trust each other with the parts that can be hurt...

...when we are seeing and being seen for who we really are.

Intimacy is bridging the
distance we make to stay safe...

...giving up the power
we hold over each other.

Intimacy is the
moment when we touch.

Intimacy does sound great...

...but the truth is it's terrifying.

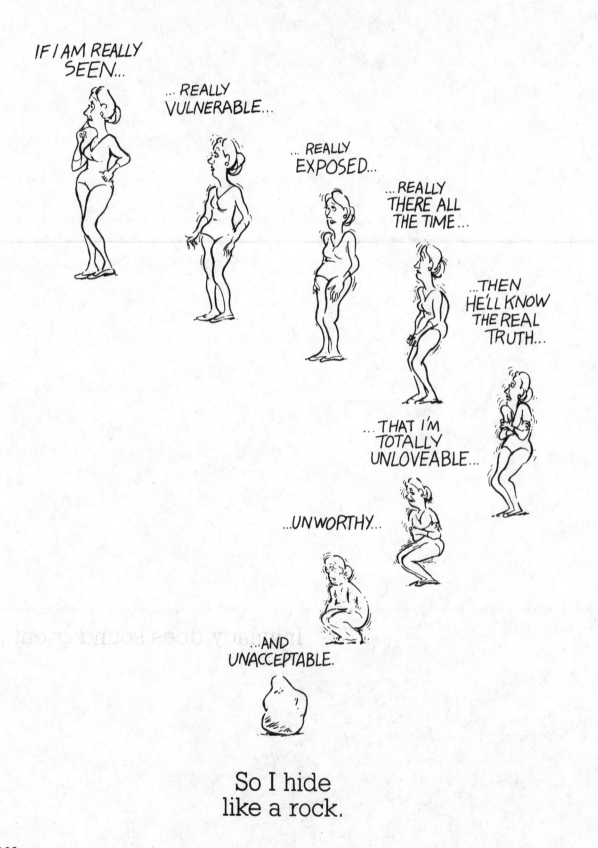

IF I AM REALLY SEEN...

... REALLY VULNERABLE...

... REALLY EXPOSED...

...REALLY THERE ALL THE TIME...

...THEN HE'LL KNOW THE REAL TRUTH...

...THAT I'M TOTALLY UNLOVEABLE...

...UNWORTHY...

...AND UNACCEPTABLE.

So I hide
like a rock.

And who
wants a rock?

So I become
unloveable
as I feared
I might.

There is no safe or easy way to intimacy. The mutual rewards require a mutual risk.

Intimacy will elude the dancers if both are not ready to take real risks at the same time. We must look at the steps we think we are taking toward intimacy...

...are they truly vulnerable and mutual?

Some feel intimacy
is giving...

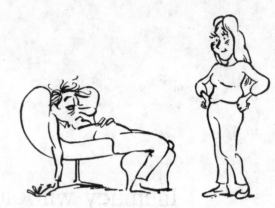

Some feel it is sharing
their deepest feelings...

But giving and sharing are
easy risks when you know your
partner isn't really there...

...like those who
risk intimacy
only when it's safe.

Some feel safest when
their partners are unavailable.

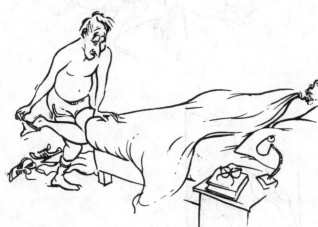

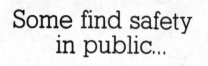

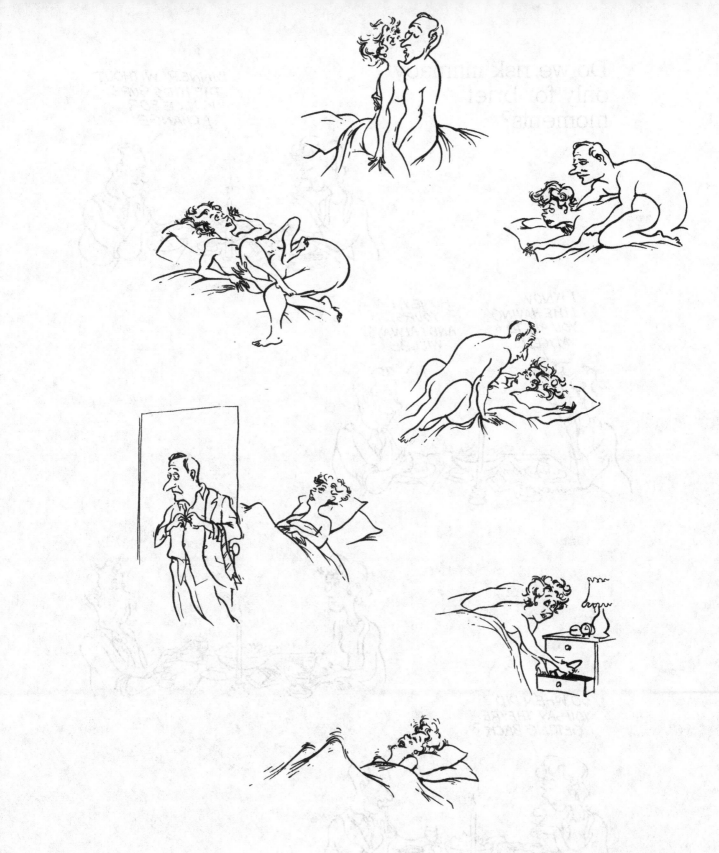

...others in
solitude.

Do we risk intimacy only for brief moments?

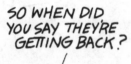

Can we see each other only after a big fight?

Do we need
to manufacture a
crisis to get close?

Does our intimacy happen only at set times?

...or are we open for
the moment to happen
spontaneously?

There is a delicate balance
between our need
for intimacy...

...and our fear of it.

Too often our fears
drive us to positions
of safety...

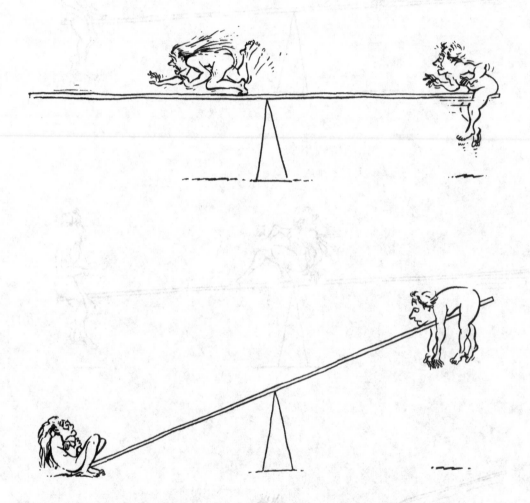

...invulnerable positions
of power and distance.

How do we create the intimacy we need to bring our dance to life again?

Although
the Two-Step
is a dance for
two, it takes only
one to initiate change.

When **you** stop playing your
old role you set the stage for a
new level of intimacy.

In taking this new step,
   you put yourself at risk...

...there is no way to know how
   your partner may respond.

If your partner won't make the
risk mutual the dance is dead.

Here we come up against the basic myth most of us share – that we can be whole only through union with another.

This myth keeps us constantly looking to the other to satisfy our needs – to fill our holes.

It locks us into old unhappy roles and relationships, unable to risk the prospect of being alone. Many admit: "I'd rather be in a bad relationship than none at all."

But we are each alone. No relationship and no amount of intimacy can save us from that.

We each enjoy our peaks, orgasms, and fantasies...endure our pains, needs and sorrows without ever really being able to have another know what it is for us.

...Accepting our aloneness
while in a relationship
is a big new step.

If the distance in our relationship bothers me...if the power between us feels unequal...if our needs for intimacy don't match – then I may have to deal with some of my fears about getting closer, being vulnerable, more intimate, or being alone.

Dealing with my fears that keep me stuck in old ruts is a new step.

For the SEEKER to be pursued
and wanted...as he has always
said he wanted to be...

...he pays a price. He feels
cold and distant, missing his old
hunger for the other.

The SOUGHT in switching to SEEKER also pays a price. She steps down from aloofness and being "desired" and becomes vulnerable as she moves toward wanting the other.

When we face our fears
together we become
mutually vulnerable.

Honesty creates
new intimacy.

As we see each other's
pain, our rigid roles of
SEEKER and SOUGHT
can soften...

WOULDST THOU HAVE ME
TRADE MY TOWER FOR
A PEDESTAL?
 I FEAR, BRAVE KNIGHT,
I SHALL NEVER LIVE UP
TO THY LOFTY IDEALS.
 IF ONLY THOU WOULDST
CAST ASIDE THY LYRE
AND CEASE THY
WRETCHED SONG —
MAYHAPS I WOULD FIND
COURAGE TO RISK A
TRYST WITH THEE.

...and we can switch.

But we don't just dance
off into the sunset.

One intimate exchange doesn't transform our whole relationship. Every step of the dance brings new fears for both of us.

The transition
from intimacy back
to SEEKER and SOUGHT
roles is difficult because
intimacy is hard to give up.

Many people think that an intimate relationship means being intimate all the time. Intimacy is forever, "happily ever after," isn't it?...

No! Being naked, vulnerable, and exposed is intense. An hour of intimacy is a very long time. An intimate moment cannot last all day.

Giving up an
intimate moment
involves fear of
losing your partner...

...and that can
lead to power
struggles.

Only when
we let go can we
find out if we are
truly wanted.

Will he choose me if
I give him room to seek?

Only when we
can freely
come...

...and go...

...can we
more freely
come again...

...and
again.

The hope for our dance lies
in our willingness to be
honest about our needs and
fears –

– to trust and **risk**.

Every time I risk myself
by seeking I am
freer to give.

Each time I risk
myself by being
sought I am
freer to
receive.

Switching
freely back
and forth...

...allows a new
security
between us.

I can
SEEK now...

...knowing I'll be
SOUGHT later.

Moving in and out of intimacy,
acknowledging the goodness
and scariness of what we share...

...and the loneliness of
the spaces in between...

...is the best that we can do.

When we do, our
Two-Step is a
vital dance.

REALLY DANCING...

In our relationships most of us become accustomed to seeing the other as withholding something intentionally, or chasing us with demands that we cannot meet. We become defensive and it is difficult to see the pain, the struggle of the other. Yet in seeing that pain, and the fears that drive our partner, we soften. We come out of our trenches and into a space in which neither blames or demands, into compassion and a more realistic assessment of how we can be with each other while respecting the needs we have for distance and power.

A tall order – is it hopeless then?

No, not hopeless. Difficult and painful at times, but not hopeless – and worth the struggle. For in the end it is seeing and being seen, being known and held dear to another that makes life and death easier.

We are not in this dance to keep endlessly seeking and being sought. In spite of our fears, we are all striving for intimacy more often, wanting to be able to stay closer longer. The roles of SEEKER and SOUGHT will not disappear, but we can risk playing the less familiar role and become more comfortable and less destructive in our switching. We will continue to experience our needs for distance and power in our relationships, yet we can learn to meet these needs in ways that are satisfying to us and acceptable to our partner.

Ultimately it is our willingness to work on our relationships – to risk, to be honest, and to be vulnerable that can transform a tired Two-Step into a dance that returns joy and meaning to our relationships and our lives.